The Graywolf Poetry Re/View Series

James L. White (1936–1981) combined the rhetorical strategies of Deep Image poetry with a startling emotional directness and a frank treatment of sexual longing. White's work has remained a significant influence for a number of gay American poets, but his consideration of desire and loneliness reaches beyond any categories of identity. His singular achievement, the posthumously published *The Salt Ecstasies*, is reprinted here along with a previously unpublished poem and a powerful autobiographical prose fragment.

> Mark Doty, Series Editor

The Graywolf Poetry Re/View Series brings essential books of contemporary American poetry back into the light of print. Each volume—chosen by series editor Mark Doty—is introduced by a poet who comes to the work with a passionate admiration. The Graywolf Poetry Re/View Series offers all-but-lost masterworks of recent American poetry to a new generation of readers.

Volumes in the Graywolf Poetry Re/View Series:
   Collected Poems by Lynda Hull,
      with an introduction by Yusef Komunyakaa
   Letters to a Stranger by Thomas James,
      with an introduction by Lucie Brock-Broido
   The Salt Ecstasies by James L. White.
      with an introduction by Mark D

Sleep

Let me sleep for us all
further than our aging.
To the elmed season,
sun found and cradled
within the browning shell.

We'll sleep tonight
who've tightened nerves into years
with our faces of electricity.

Let's sleep into a flesh fall nearly innocent
where warmth is brought by skin and breath.
We'll wrap our hair into the swirled white
of hill line and fur.

Traveler,
gone too far,
return and rest.

I think this as a
Preface poem.

James L. White
The Salt Ecstasies

Graywolf Press

This publication is made possible by funding provided in part by a grant from the Minnesota State Arts Board, through an appropriation by the Minnesota State Legislature, a grant from the National Endowment for the Arts, and private funders. Significant support has also been provided by Target; the McKnight Foundation; and other generous contributions from foundations, corporations, and individuals. To these organizations and individuals we offer our heartfelt thanks.

The Salt Ecstasies was originally published by Graywolf Press, 1982.

"An Autobiographical Fragment" and "Whitefish Lake, Late Summer, 1978" appeared in *Tin House*, along with Mark Doty's introductory essay.

Published by Graywolf Press
250 Third Avenue North, Suite 600
Minneapolis, Minnesota 55401
All rights reserved.

www.graywolfpress.org

Published in the United States of America

ISBN 978-1-55597-561-6

2 4 6 8 9 7 5 3 1
First Graywolf Printing, 2010

Library of Congress Control Number: 2010920767

Cover design: Kyle G. Hunter

Cover photo: Ellen Hawley

Contents

UNCOLLECTED WORK

Introduction

Sometime toward the end of the 1990s, I went for a walk in downtown Minneapolis, on Hennepin Avenue, in a neighborhood that seemed at the end of one era in its life and not yet quite launched on the next. There were, and now and then still are, zones like this in all large American cities. Banks of winking yellow lightbulbs around the doors of a movie theater. A porn shop with booths of continuously rolling films on screens smaller than a sheet of typing paper—continuous, that is, if you fed tokens into a slot. Wig shops, pawnshops, liquor stores with exaggerated metal grates over the windows, protecting stacks of vodka bottles. Bus stations. Tattoos, discount electronics, smoke shops, bars. Unforgettably, on one corner, a ruined shadowbox window display: against a backdrop of cracked and dusty mirror, a display of false teeth.

Such neighborhoods were zones of permission of many sorts. In Boston, in the Combat Zone, the ceilings of the city's oldest gay bar were decorated for every holiday, swathed in enough ribbons of crepe paper to keep what must have been a faltering industry alive. In Providence, right across the street from the renovated civic theater where touring companies mounted Broadway shows for the pleasures of suburban visitors, steam from the baths' laundry poured out all night from second-story vents, roiling in the winter air. Such neighborhoods seemed doomed, at the twentieth century's end, giving way to new urban lofts and condo conversions, or the kind of managed shopping/dining/residential complexes the developers were calling "lifestyle centers." There was plenty not to be nostalgic about—grit, danger, the evidence of human suffering on display—and yet those places were also haunted, in part because they'd been free zones for gay men for at least half a century, parts of the city where desire could play out almost freely. That's why, walking on Hennepin on the freezing early winter morning, I thought, I'm walking in a James White poem.

White's poems inhabit these decaying urban spaces that are at once understood as tawdry and utterly beautiful, steeped as they are in the burnishing chemical bath of desire:

> The Union Station sleeps like a defunct whale
> and I join its echoing space to think of caskets settling.
> I've returned to dust where the peeling signs read:
> REMEMBER ALL DEPARTURES ARE CHANGEABLE.

Or:

> Tell the one about an hour before darkness
> in your room above the Bangcock Massage Parlour.

Or:

> Transients loiter in downtown parks with
> the stillness of foxes.

Or his own body grown "older than the dirty magazines in the dirty shops / he so revered." Or, finally:

> The neon lights up tit-pink:
>> and the night
>> and the night
>> *and the night!*

This is the pre-Stonewall landscape of American gay men. I don't mean "Stonewall" as an event here (history is never that simple, that a single watershed changes everything) but as short-hand for a process of transformation in American culture, still underway, that would bring us out from the late-night allure of downtowns like this one and into the light of day. James L. White's poems predate this process, even though his single great book, *The Salt Ecstasies*, appeared in 1982. That year, the year after White died, may have been thirteen years after the riots in the West Village, but this was Minnesota, and White was in his forties, raised in Indiana—and was thus in essence, a citizen of another era. Or nearly so. What *had* changed for him was what might be spoken. In a remarkable fragment of autobiographical prose—published for the first time in this volume—he writes:

> Looking back on it I wish I'd had the courage not to have
> gone to the Army. To have gone to jail, but I was too afraid.
> I was afraid because I was gay and for me saying I was gay
> was something you didn't do in the fifties.

By the late 1970s, as the poems collected here make abundantly clear, White had found the courage to articulate a life of desire, and the particular character that his longing had leant to his experience. These bold and indelible poems would open new prospects for many poets to come.

Which is not to say, of course, that American poems about gay male experience didn't exist. Of course they did, well before the debut of White's landmark book. (A posthumous appearance, sadly: the poet had died of heart disease a few months before, with the corrected galleys of *The Salt Ecstasies* on his bedside table.) There were poems aplenty that chronicled same-sex relations, but they didn't work quite like these did.

I was twenty-six in 1980, which was young for a gay man in those days, perhaps more so than is the case now—and I probably was, in any case, younger at that age than most, still finding my way toward a life that felt centered authentically in my own desire. I'd been married early, and I'd lived a life as a poet before I was a "gay poet," whatever that meant. As I came out, and began to admit more of my own experience into my poetry—(Which of those came first? Hard now exactly to say.)—I was casting about for models, reading everything I could get my hands on. It seemed to me then that the poems by gay men I read divided themselves into two primary sorts.

There were first of all the poems which foregrounded sexual life; if erotic behavior is the point of difference, these odes and pleas seemed to say, then let's put that in the foreground, let's use poetry as a ground for the celebration of what's been so long condemned. These were collected in anthologies like *The Male Muse* and published in gay magazines. They might be sexy as all get out (like Allen Ginsberg's unforgettable "Master" poem), but they seldom satisfied. Ironically, as they tried to include what had been erased from the poetry of the past, they wound up excluding so much of experience—centering as they did on the delicious fire of lust, which, translated into language, often has an air of the auto-erotic about it that may not leave much room for the reader.

The *other* gay poets were all about style, a high-gloss, witty surface that signified—through its modes of joking, its interest in the world of high art, its elegantly arcane subjects, and its intensely wrought formality. I loved those poems, when I could find my way into them, but I wasn't sure I could write them. I was a kid from suburban Tucson who'd been to a state school, and the empyrean regions of culture evoked in those poems seemed like a foreign atmosphere to me, indeed. (Later on, I'd write poems of my own with a lush vocabulary and references to Mozart's operas and Keats's letters, but I had to be forty and in another frame of mind entirely to do so.) Richard Howard tells a wonderful joke about giving a reading with James Merrill in International Falls, Minnesota. Afterwards, they were asked about their feelings about regionalism—then a hot topic in the arts. Their region, after all, was the rarefied air of high art; what could they possibly say? Later, JM is supposed to have turned to Richard and said, "Well, my dear, this is what happens when the Great Plains meet the Great Fancies."

So those were the available models, or at least the most visible ones: unbridled horniness versus wittily elegant erudition. Even the perennially refreshing Frank O'Hara seemed finally to point toward sexuality more via style than by substance. That seemed to be the dichotomy: you could have homosexual substance in poems, or you could have a signifying style. Was there any middle ground to be found? (Curiously that "middle ground" might be the new space of a gay middle class, which one could argue hadn't really existed till very recently. You might be a privileged gay man, but when you went out to the bars or the piers you entered the demimonde, that battered night-zone on Hennepin. Now I know younger, out gay couples who are doctors and professors and therapists and you name it; I can honestly say, back in 1980, in Des Moines, I didn't know anyone like that.)

White's poems, when I found them, would strike an entirely different register. He was steeped in the poetics of the Deep Image; he'd clearly read Robert Bly and W. S. Merwin and Galway Kinnell, the poets I loved best in those days. Probably the strongest influence in *The Salt Ecstasies* is the work of James Wright, with its straightforward syntax, plain diction, and emotional availability tied to a faith in the power of the image to convey feeling and meaning. You can hear an echo of Wright in White's marvelous weddings of a direct revelation of feeling with an observation of the natural world:

> In this joyous season I know my heart won't die
> as you and the milk pods open their centers
> like a first snow in its perfection of light.

Wright was a master, of course, of perfectly placed rhetorical moves; his best-known poems follow a chain of evocations of the physical world with a sudden, striking statement that somehow manages to feel both unexpected and inevitable. White clearly learned from this, and it shows especially in his marvelous endings. The conclusion to the poem I've just quoted, "Skin Movers," for instance:

> Good love is like this.
> Even the smell of baked bread won't make it better,
> this being out of myself for a while.

But White's endings do something different from Wright's splashy final gestures. Whereas "I have wasted my life" or "Come up to me, love, out of the river, or I will come down to you" have a sweeping finality and forcefulness about them, White somehow manages to make his conclusions both poignant and offhand at once. It's that casual quality ("I just have to stop" or "you wear it broken") that gives these endings such an unmistakable sense of authenticity. That is, they are heartbroken in that everyday way we recognize; they are the exhalation of a sorrow held so long it's become as ordinary as it is sharp.

White managed to do some things in his poems that other practitioners of the Deep Image mode did not. For one thing, the poems are frankly sexual—homosexual in their inclinations, of course, but their open voicing of a craving for whatever solace might be found in another body seems to me itself a departure from the period style. That openness seems to draw in its wake other forms of disclosure. The speaker in these poems is overweight, desperately lonely, grateful for whatever scrap of joy and affection sex will bring him, and he understands that he is as much a victim of his city as he is its celebrant. And yet it's exactly right that the title of this book contains the word *ecstasies*, since here the most extraordinary pleasure (communion, surrender, all of what Rebecca Brown has called "the gifts of the body") is also inseparable from desolation.

I would like to point toward one poem in particular that seems to me White's masterwork, and as affecting and unlikely a poem as any from the second half of the century we have just seen to a close. "Making Love to Myself" begins with its title's bold gesture. Men don't usually "make love" to themselves; they jerk off, or name the autoerotic act in some similarly blunt phrase. The title not only posits for us a masturbating speaker—surely no subject position from which we expect a poet to speak—but that the act has a character or flavor somehow set apart from what we've come to expect from men.

> When I do it, I remember how it was with us.
> Then my hands remember too,
> and you're with me again, just the way it was.
>
> After work when you'd come in and
> turn the TV off and sit on the edge of the bed,
> filling the room with gasoline smell from your overalls,
> trying not to wake me which you always did.
> I'd breathe out long and say,
> 'Hi Jess, you tired baby?'
> You'd say not so bad and rub my belly,
> not after me really, just being sweet,
> and I always thought I'd die a little
> because you smelt like burnt leaves or woodsmoke.
>
> We were poor as Job's turkey but we lived well—
> the food, a few good movies, good dope, lots of talk,
> lots of you and me trying on each other's skin.

That's such a sweet evocation of a gone relationship, and it situates these lovers so clearly in the world; it's clear that Jess is a working man, that there's an easy tenderness to their coupling, and that it's one of those moments in a life when the lack of resource matters hardly a bit; these two men have all they need. There's also perhaps a subtle suggestion that their sexual relationship may matter a bit more to the speaker than it does to Jess, who's "not after me really, just being sweet," while that speaker's own longing comes blazing through to us in one of White's signature moments, when a bit of sensory description is linked to a naked declaration: "and I always thought I'd die a little / because you smelt like burnt leaves or woodsmoke." That's an unforgettable gesture, and it's the point in the poem when the past tense suddenly feels alive with ache. And it's here that the eros promised by the title has somehow slipped out of focus, as memory supplies context for this desire, and lust leads to memory that wounds. The speaker reclaims his desire in the next stanza ("lots of you and me trying on each other's skin") and again in the couplet that follows:

> What a sweet gift this is,
> done with my memory, my cock and hands.

In 1982, I'd never read a poem like this (I am not sure that I have since, now that I think about it). The diction of sex is fraught with peril. Clinical or anatomical terms are resistant to lyricism. Euphemism, with its penchant for geographical metaphor, tends to the coy and shopworn. And casual speech generally leads directly to porn, which raises other sorts of tonal problems. Therefore it seems a minor miracle that the word "cock" sits so harmoniously in this line. The small shock of it is perfect against the potentially sentimental "sweet gift," and the line pulls us back to the title, reminding us that the speaker is busy with his hands, even though they must keep slowing and losing their intention as the poem's process of remembering underscores a swelling sense of loss. (Swelling, if you will forgive the joke, more than anything else in sight in this proto-elegy, one of whose subjects is surely the deflation of eros.)

But, inevitably, desire again slips away—or perhaps it's more accurate to say that what is desired—to remain connected, to hold together—changes as the poem continues:

> Sometimes I'd wake up wondering if I should fix
> coffee for us before work,
> almost thinking you're here again, almost seeing
> your work jacket on the chair.
>
> I wonder if you remember what
> we promised when you took the job in Laramie?
> Our way of staying with each other.
> We promised there'd always be times
> when the sky was perfectly lucid,
> that we could remember each other through that.
> You could remember me at my worktable
> or in the all-night diners,
> though we'd never call or write.
>
> I just have to stop here Jess.
> I just have to stop.

Laramie, of course, is never *that* far away, though I doubt that White could have chosen a town that somehow sounded more distant from anywhere. Why wouldn't these men call or write? Surely because they understand the limitation of their union; I imagine Jess being ready to move on, and the speaker bravely participating in this romantic narrative of sustained memory.

Or maybe not. Both men may have felt ready to move on, and perhaps it's the gift of memory that revises the speaker's estimation of this love; is it in retrospect that the these old days have been burnished? Here I think of Cavafy, whose memories of decades-old sexual encounters "come to rest" in his poems. The difference of course, is that the Greek poet praises sensuality, as if it's a god himself who's appeared to him in the bodies of handsome young men. None of those men are named, in his work, and few have individual characteristics other than a linen suit or a sensuous mouth. And though Jess is economically evoked on the page, there's something indelible about those overalls, some quality of the specific and irreplaceable in this relation that makes the poem the wounding thing it is. Here Cavafy's gesture of erotic recapitulation seems to have married James Wright's vulnerability.

A quality nowhere more on display than in the startling final lines. Stop what, we might ask? Stop speaking this poem, because the memory of that man is bringing me to orgasm? Stop speaking the poem, or stop masturbating, because I'm going to weep? Or should we read it in a more general way: stop wounding myself with this memory, give up this attachment? Or even in a more general way: I want to stop being I, I've had enough, I can't live in this pain.

All of the above, of course, which is the genius of those lines, which send us right back to the beginning of the poem again.

Earlier, I called "Making Love to Myself" a proto-elegy. I'd like to suggest that it provides a sort of template for the sorts of poems that gay men were compelled to write a decade later, when the epidemic began to send a generation of lovers irrecoverably to the Laramies of Elysium. It's an elegiac mode that recognizes and identifies the difficult territory where eros and grief overlap, where tenderness is charged with physical fellow-feeling, where the absence of the body is inscribed as a charm for and an evocation of the vanished and lingering soul.

I have pressed *The Salt Ecstasies* into the hands of many young gay male poets over the years. I will never forget one in particular, a man in his twenties who'd form strong political and social relationships with lesbians, and who desperately sought a sense of community with other men—who made him, it's fair to say, nervous. He hated the book. He objected to the speaker's seemingly intractable loneliness, to his night-realm of bars and baths and bus station, to his use of the phrase "tit-pink" (an example of gay men's misogyny, he thought), to the poem in which the "colored girl" gives the speaker a cigarette. He hated the shame that informed the book; White's poems did not affirm him; they did not offer hope. He wanted to simply step around shame, not to confront it and go through it. I think now what he truly could not abide was the portrayal of a fiercely unhappy man, the idea that a life of expressed desire might not lead one to an earthly paradise of harmonious relation.

I doubt that any of the young gay male poets I know today would have that reaction; further and further from the closet, we come to an increasingly complex understanding of the power and failure of desire, the ways that liberation isn't a cure for loneliness or soul-ache or despair. Not that we'd trade this hard-won freedom for anything; it's simply that we're as free to be as sexually confused, as bowled over by longing, as uncertain as anyone else is.

In 2008, I visited the One Archive in Los Angeles, a repository of gay and lesbian history housed in a 1960s school building near USC. I'd made an appointment in advance, and the good-natured and dapper librarian on duty showed me to a table in the middle of what must have been the old school cafeteria/gymnasium, quite like the spaces in a couple of schools I remember: high ceilings, skylights, tables that fold down from the walls. I think at one school I attended this was called (ugh) "the cafetorium."

By the time I settled in, the librarian was already on his way back to my table with two black plastic file boxes with handles on top, the sort you might buy to keep your tax records in. The sensations that came flooding in, when I opened them, were complicated ones.

First, there was the odd sense of entering into a privacy. White had been dead for twenty-five years, and here, neatly lined up, were his journals, a set of composition books. He'd collaged the covers of most of them with bits of paper—wrappers from tea, fragments of text, bits of watercolor or magic marker scribbles. Inside: photographs of Jim and his friends in diners or living rooms, strips of pictures from photo booths, and a great deal of handwritten text. Most of it, I discovered as I began to read, was the sort of outpouring of everything that's wrong that one does in a notebook—anger at the self about smoking, weight, failed relationships, anger at others about snubs or spurned affection, outcries about the injustices of rejection and literary reputation. It was painful to read, the stuff you wouldn't want to survive you— and in between these bouts of venting, there were the scrawled drafts of poems I love, many of the poems that would become *The Salt Ecstasies* germinating here, some of them almost complete.

And then there was the strange sensation of immediate presence. All you had to do was open these boxes and begin to read and here was a man alive, wounded, hungry, lusting, greedy, and sore. I felt like he'd walked into the room with me. I wondered who'd read these last, how long since these boxes were opened? And presence, of course, makes one think of time, and of disappearance. And what might I want, of my own, to wind up in such a storage case, a quarter century after I'm gone?

Along with the daunting pleasure of meeting a dead man that afternoon, I found three particular treasures, which are published here for the first time. The first is twenty-two pages of typescript, a fragment of autobiographical prose, dictated or written over several days in 1979. The text suggests that White may have begun this by dictating into a tape recorder, reflecting on his life, and then moved at some point to the typewriter.

The manuscript is clearly unrevised; it's laden with repetitions, digressions, and bits and pieces out of order he must have intended to work with at some later date. It's a remarkable document, quite direct and apparently artless yet very much a made thing, a potent testament. Because White himself never revised it, as far as I know, I have allowed myself a free hand as an editor, removing material that seemed to me extraneous, cutting extra words and repetitions. I reasoned that, had I left such material in rough shape myself, I'd be grateful for intervention. And I wanted the power of White's sentences to shine through without distraction.

The second discovery is a poem, "Whitefish Lake, Late Summer, 1978." It exists only in White's handwriting, and I found several versions. The one reprinted here was labeled "Draft 3," and it may well be among the poet's final works.

The third uncollected piece is a poem titled "Sleep." White wrote, at the bottom of a typescript of the poem placed at the beginning of a draft of *The Salt Ecstasies*, "I think this as a preface poem." Perhaps the poem was removed from this position because of its valedictory tone, but it is certainly a fitting conclusion to this volume.

I don't think I can evoke, here, the pathos and force of White's notebooks, the evidence of a life pasted onto the page beside those coruscating or self-castigating or lyric words. Perhaps I can give just one resonant example. On a page in the tenth journal, from April 1981, is pasted an advertising card from a bar. At the upper left is a photo of a black woman in a luxuriant wig, in ¾ profile, and beside her in large cursive the message:

FLO GAVIN
At the piano
With Dewey Duewson on Bass
Pleased to honor your requests
Tuesday thru Saturday
The Meridian Pub

And underneath this, in White's own handwriting:

The Asylum of Unquestioned Dying
There are places of sexual regret where touching another is
simply loneliness being acted out.

Perhaps that juxtaposition says more, at last, about who Jim White must have been than I ever could.

A few acknowledgments and notes are in order: my gratitude to Kate Green, James White's friend and literary executor, and David Wojahn, a friend of the poet who preserved various drafts and uncollected poems, as well as to Graywolf for the original publication of this book. And to Jeff Shotts for his continued assistance and good spirits, and to the One Archive in Los Angeles for their important contribution to the preservation of American gay and lesbian history.

James L. White actually published several small-press volumes during his lifetime: *Divorce Proceedings* (1972), *A Crow's Story of Deer* (1974), *The Del Rio Hotel* (1975). There are also several uncollected poems that appeared in magazines, presumably work that White either excluded from *The Salt Ecstasies* (1982) or intended to collect later on in another volume. I have chosen to include only the final book and three previously unpublished pieces here because I wanted to make the best possible case for White's work. He is a poet who came into his own at mid-life; in these pages, his accomplishment is extraordinarily visible.

Mark Doty

The Salt Ecstasies

For Kate Green

Whosoever liveth with these scars
shall dwell outside the camp.

Leviticus

An Ordinary Composure

I question what poetry will tremble the wall into hearing or tilt the stone angel's slight wings at words of the past like a memory caught in elms. We see nothing ahead. My people and I lean against great medical buildings with news of our predicted death, and give up mostly between one and three in the morning, never finding space large enough for a true departure, so our eyes gaze earthward, wanting to say something simple as *the meal's too small: I want more.* Then we empty from a room on Intensive Care into the sea, releasing our being into the slap of waves.

Poems break down here at the thought of arms never coupling into full moons by holding those we love again, and so we resort to the romantic: a white horse set quivering like a slab of marble into dancing flesh.

Why remember being around a picnic table over at Brookside Park? We played softball that afternoon. My mother wore her sweater even in the summer because of the diabetes. Night blackened the lake like a caught breath. We packed things up. I think I was going to school that fall or a job somewhere. Michael'd go to Korea. Before we left I hit the torn softball into the lake and Michael said, 'You can't do that for shit James Lee.'

Going back I realized the picnic was for us. It started raining in a totally different way, knowing we'd grow right on up into wars and trains and deaths and loving people and leaving them and being left and being alone.

That the way of my life, the ordinary composure of loving, loneliness and death, and too these prayers at the waves, the white horse shimmering, bringing it toward us out of the coldest marble.

Gatherings

1. New Light

I've been dying to go back
through dust, hymns, and the photos of death.
The Union Station sleeps like a defunct whale
and I join its echoing space to think of caskets settling.
I've returned to dust where the peeling signs read:
REMEMBER ALL DEPARTURES ARE CHANGEABLE
BE SURE YOU ARE IN THE CORRECT TIME.
I want to sleep now
in an afternoon dream pushing 'now' away to die completely
as stone or heart
or rising wind.

I want to dream beyond this aloneness,
to feel him carry me through the wind that is rising.
My father in his white strolling suit.
I ride his shoulders into the greening
light of this damp time.

We take flowers in the morning,
my father, bold as God,
mother in her withering step,
in her withering white,
and me in boyhood with a sword of lilacs.

In this dream my people live forever.
We carry the flowers of waltzing light
into rising wind, through into spring.

We, who are going on a trip.

2. Memorial Day

'Memorial Day, 1940, Logansport, Indiana.'
is written on the decayed photo I keep.
'Estell, Rose, Roscoe,
Marie by the Hudson with *the boy*.'

They tell me to wave to my aunts
though I don't know what wave means.
I stare like a sullen disease into the camera
with my pale hand floating upward, locked
in that motion forever—
my old man's face like a hospital fart
my ribs mean as a prediction of collapse
my burnt eyes questioning the graves
my mother in her withering cotton
my father's strolling suit.

And because nothing is ever answered
I think of lizards going into the earth
and know like the knots of my back
what anguish lay ahead for us
and stare at that anguish
and stare at nothing at all.

In these small years I stay near my mother
who smells of Lily of the Valley and damp earth
so unlike the men who open life with their blazing shares.
My mother binds vision, silence and pain in her flesh,
and I know in her small turning that all our measured ways
throb toward death.

My aunts are in their eternal black,
placing peonies and little flags on the graves.
I wave to these women, not knowing the word.
Women whose casket lids have long since closed them
into perfect darkness.
Still, my little boy's hand
holding them above ground forever
waving, waving over their graves.

3. Losing Light

'Wave good-bye now, we're going!'
I don't know what going or good-bye mean
and twist my face into a screw.
I leave a place I can't remember
except for an awakening spring
and a river veering near a graveyard perhaps.

We enter the Indianapolis Union Station
early in the evening.
Last sun pours through the corroded windows above us,
lighting the filthy terminal.
My father is slightly drunk and quiet.
My mother is breathless
and I know we are all dying in the train calls,
the old picnic basket and brown paper bags.
I know we are all dying there.

4. Lost Light

Shall we.
Shall we gather at the river.
My mother and father laugh in the early evening
and I know the dream is nearly ended.
. . . at the beautiful, beautiful river.
They rise in lines of kindly light skyward, toward the sun,
at the beautiful, beautiful river.

I wake in lost light
to hear doors echo above the failed day,
and wear the absence
like an old ticket saved for home, though not returning.

I wake and cannot find the river,
nor can I even remember the beautiful, beautiful river.
I've traveled long enough to be old from this,
from seeking the river, the beautiful river.
I cannot find the river, the beautiful river,
or the beautiful way home.

I'd Trade These Words

I'd trade these words on the spot
to see you again
in the cold practice room above the city.
Old madame what's-her-name playing for class.

My God Marina, it's you at the *barre*
with old leg-warmers and fine perfume!
I'd trade these words
to be a soundless angel again
pulling my muscles into music.

When too much has gone shabby in my life
I can still see you
so many years after your Achilles tendon
exploded on the Spanish tour,
so many years after my legs stopped jumping.

Do you remember that night after work
we went out with your husband?
We'd done 'The Waltzes Noble and Sentimental'
and it ended with my head resting on your breast.
Your husband and I were like two suitors
with the same lover.
He suddenly touched your cheek
and in that awkward silence I thought,
'I know you more.
I know your body more.'
We had sung the space together
with our design to break each
audience's heart as finally as our own.

What I wouldn't give for that cold practice room
and me lifting you without regard
goddamn it, perfectly
into our timeless air.

for MARINA CHAPMAN DOYLE

Lying in Sadness

Moon to my earth come from some other space
so totally white at our evening meal,
wearing a coat that will not last the year,
I love you completely as salt.

Tell the one about an hour before darkness
in your room above the Bangcock Massage Parlour.
The one where pain rises with the bread,
filling you with its yeasting smell.

It's dark.
You exhale a fist of memory.
I love you like weathering wood
in a room of empty pianos.

When you return to something you love,
it's already beyond repair.
You wear it broken.

The First Time

Sometimes I'm their first.
Sweet, sweet men.
I light candles, burn the best incense.
Make them think it's some kind of temple
and it rather is.

Like this guy who hauled parts for a living,
whatever the hell that means.
He was like caught light through glass,
and so the candles and the incense.
What would you do with a new colt?

He touched my body the way shadows fall
from an old subject he'd buried,
and he looked at me without fear.

Sweet guy.
So sweet I became really shy and hot
so I had to move easy.
Wouldn't you?
What do you do when it's someone's first time?
I try to clean up my act.
Make it into a first rate number
so he knows he's been with someone.

We're bunglers when it's really good:
bow legs, pimply backs, scrawny chest hair,
full of mistakes and good intentions.
And it doesn't have to do with women.
They're fine too.
Just some understanding between two men.

Making Love to Myself

When I do it, I remember how it was with us.
Then my hands remember too,
and you're with me again, just the way it was.

After work when you'd come in and
turn the TV off and sit on the edge of the bed,
filling the room with gasoline smell from your overalls,
trying not to wake me which you always did.
I'd breathe out long and say,
'Hi Jess, you tired baby?'
You'd say not so bad and rub my belly,
not after me really, just being sweet,
and I always thought I'd die a little
because you smelt like burnt leaves or woodsmoke.

We were poor as Job's turkey but we lived well—
the food, a few good movies, good dope, lots of talk,
lots of you and me trying on each other's skin.

What a sweet gift this is,
done with my memory, my cock and hands.

Sometimes I'd wake up wondering if I should fix
coffee for us before work,
almost thinking you're here again, almost seeing
your work jacket on the chair.

I wonder if you remember what
we promised when you took the job in Laramie?
Our way of staying with each other.
We promised there'd always be times

when the sky was perfectly lucid,
that we could remember each other through that.
You could remember me at my worktable
or in the all-night diners,
though we'd never call or write.

I just have to stop here Jess.
I just have to stop.

Taken to a Room

Taken to a room with you asleep,
I want to touch you there
beneath the galaxy of star quilt.
You unfold letting me into the warmth
and everything rises from my dick to my breath
saying we are here.

In my mind I kiss you away, your beard
and earring, the tattooed heart of Christ
on your chest, and remember
a prison boy named Rubio,
then I kiss down on all of you.

Now I'm taken to a room fully awake
and warned my imagination is out of hand.
They show me a solo screaming bed
and quilt of fallen stars.
I pant hard over this poem
wanting to write your body again.

In this totally conscious poem
you're gone and they unplug my systems,
my heart, my lungs, my brains.
In front of the crowd they flash blinding lights
on my crotch and neuter me down to a smile.

I try to think about your eyes
and remember nothing.
Now they drag me off to the next room
where the real work begins.

Summer News

Transients loiter in downtown parks with
the stillness of foxes.
One smiles as if I know him near a fountain
in his center of light,
wearing a faded shirt like summer news.

His body invites conversation.
They threaten tornados through the city as
hunters and prey agree on common shelter.
The storm enters our skin gathering
as we begin the familiar gestures.

In his room I speak of death, its promise of ending.
He undresses me, telling me how tired I am,
that friends have brought me their truths all day.
He seems as beautiful as I wish my life was
in the boiling light of our slight sweating.

Now the old blues
before the bad gin and storm.
We vow total selfishness
and we begin to touch

and we begin to rain . . .

The Salt Ecstasies

Salt me down where love was
on a blue burn to remember the real pain.
I'm worn out from my back's arch and pull,
bending like a crazy-house mirror to suit your needs
in this endless flesh revolt, trying to win
with my mouth and ass.

I want to be your yoke this time,
pushing you away in the dusty light
from gutting me to nothing, and stay
drawn in, like an old girl
after a hard Saturday night, her body
empty of carriage,
alone and complete
in the room's stillness.

I leave you first in sleep,
my breasts, my V, and hair,
then take the early bus to Laurel
away from the raw and nameless.

Some farm kid presses against my leg.
I look at the long backs of men in the fields
and doze to dream you're going through me
like winter bone, your logs of arms pushing
me down into some stifling contract with flesh
until I break free for air.

The Clay Dancer

1.

You are buried in so many places
like the scattering of diseased ivory.
The infamous motels of quick nights,
the way you like it and do it best.

The *Morning Star* says you didn't sleep well into spring
and finally gave everything away on blue paper
like the hunter's bow and ashes.

He wakes, touches himself there, looks
at the skin magazine and can't sleep.

2.

Toward the last
they said voices summoned you
to write two or three poems a day.
Did you mention the white rooms near Clairmont
or the black roses poised against the stone?
     'No.'

Then what did you write of?
     'The manner of summer suns.
     A walker to spring.
     The false myths of my bloodlines.'

Then what did you write of?
     'How I failed as a man
     or what was asked of my manhood,
     through the long distance,
     dreaming wrong.'

Then what did you write of?
     'Trains under my sleep to Dearborn and beyond.'

Then what did you write of?
     'My first time
     in that hot room.
     The guilt, the shame making it perfect.'

Then what did you write of?
     'Only what I chased.
     Dust in a hundred cities

and the blind swaying just right.
Mother hanging sheets by the steaming tub.
The bluing smell for my father's shirts.
His white Sunday strolling suit.
His never being dead enough.'

But did you mention the white rooms near Clairmont
or the black roses by the stone?
    'No, only my first bus to Demming, Texas.'

Then it must be time for you to go.

His heels click against the street as he searches for you.

3.

Do you like it this way?
Do you do it often?
Do you like the blind swaying
and the washstand and the cough
in the halls before night?
Do you like the lice-ridden pigeons
cooing their terrible vision of the wino's city?
Do you like the trembling Sunday streets and one café?
Do you like my fat body catching breath?
Do you like our sleep filling the room?
Can you stay this way a little longer
before your bus to L. A.?

He looks in the dirty movies but you're not there.

4.

The cause of death:
These white rooms await the writing of your life,
well worn and empty.

You enter the echoes
and begin notes on the highway,
the old pickup toward Burntwater
carrying the battered suitcase.

And the poem stops there finally and forever
in the long shadows of the chair
amid the faucets and kitchen smells
where silence is larger than
the room in which you write your life.

It no longer matters that he knows your address.

5.

After the last well-saved valium
you do not remember forgiving yourself
in the vomit and urine
but trying to focus on the spreading dahlias
above the bed.

6.

The man in leather is finally at your bed.
He strips down to your mother
who wanders through your cold boyhood house
giving out blankets to empty rooms.

A wheel in you forgets to breathe,
and you are dead,
and you know you are dead.

7.

Embalmer's report:
He looked like corroded alabaster on the worktable.
His old body, the cracked desert roads, older
than the courthouse square, older than the farmers
spitting their phlegm-filled days,
older than the dirty magazines in the dirty shops
in the dirty cities he so revered.

His open arteries discharged two white colts.
His childless loins repaid
the turquoise, the amber and agate.

His yellowed body finished with the flutes,
finished with the mycins of regret,
finished with the vaporizers and failures,
canceled the bromides and small dreams.
But his eyes wouldn't film
or close, saw further than they should.
Only the two colts remained,
their eyes toward still water,
the blue grass and bean blossom.

8.

What goes into heaven with you
so perfectly prepared on the pillow
like a dead satyr?
Lights from the remaining colts
or the cold cafés of November
near your turquoise hands?
The faceless loins?
The rotted coyotes?
The aged owls?
Agate temple?
Corn fire?

None.

You go without streets, songs, or hair.

9.

Here at the Del Rio, honey
your shaken steps are voided.
An anonymous patron has picked up your tab.
Your room's off the veranda.
It's quiet here except for weekends
when Reba brings the girls down for the sailors.

You look quite young in your famous blue button-down.
A sax and piano begin the waltz.
Sweet Chocolate sends you your first drink.
The neon lights up tit-pink:
    and the night
    and the night
    and the night!

Skin Movers

How still we are in sleep
as though morning holds its breath.
Our bodies rinsed with light
like soaked birch.

Half awake I travel down you again.
Crow, dark crow, we smell of burnt leaves and wine,
the night before taking crystals bitter as Jesuit Root.
Now we turn slowly in the weight of love,
the way ships move heavily between moon and sun, not lost
but like a well-piloted dream.

You speak of a river near home named Dancer's Run,
almost dust in summer that tells the story of the village.
I know your body so and kiss the star mole on your back.
Wanting more, you say yes in that miraculous way.

In this joyous season I know my heart won't die
as you and the milk pods open their centers
like a first snow in its perfection of light.

Good love is like this.
Even the smell of baked bread won't make it better,
this being out of myself for a while.

Overweight

Cooking for someone can be loaded with danger.
He'll get here at six and I'm filled with a small fear
of conversation at the table.
I always toy with the edge across my throat,
between the cabbage, the duck and coffee we stare into.

There are many ways to scream.
I've chosen the silent one
because I'm afraid of being discovered as I am, not
who he remembers 20 years ago.

I want to say things have changed since then.
I've smoked my lungs black and eaten my heart out.
Lost each leaf of hair and seen friends to their graves.

So the real talk is never said.
After a polite time he leaves a bit early.
I want to re-run dinner again
with simpler food, the apartment a little messy.
I'd like to walk right over the edge and say,
'Who we were then is fable.'
But that takes believing we're someone right now.

Instead I sit down to a second meal.
I'm famished from things left unsaid,
go to bed too early, and wake totally
at the national anthem, before the TV hisses
into blue snow.

I get up. I eat again.

Poems of Submission

1. Submission to Time

How beautiful we are when submitted fully to time,
knowing some tree from childhood crashing then to earth.
Time, the land history found in our pulse.
Land and tree rise like a woman's laughter in a bar.

See the filthy windows.
It's three in the afternoon and we are
drawn from all our fiber.
Three o'clock and the coffee's old.
A chill across our backs.

Now the tenement ages
against the paling sun across the way.
Watch the evening news.
Don't eat so much salt.
See the old man's dog,
the wind-filled street and splitting elm
from such a timeless place.

2. Submission to Pain

Yanis, my friend in the next bed cries:
tomorrow they'll cut his frozen fingers off.
He has submitted that his hands
will never know gathered dust
or circle the chipped edge of a yellow bowl,
even the perfunctory need to touch his penis.
Never to play by fingertip the lyre
of his wife's hair
or draw around slowly her nipples
into rings of heat.

Yanis, Hungarian born, fought in the '56 revolt.
The Russians left holes through which he stares
long out the hospital window:
a mother, grandmother and father.

We prowl the ward late at night
before the Percodan works.
Pretty high once, he told me in Budapest
everything becomes blue with the moon,
that it was not uncommon to see old blue horses
by his house when he was a boy.

Then he apologized,
said the narcotic made his mind odd,
odd like a poet's.

3. Submission to Death

Our loved ones, allowing them to die forever
like noticing the weakened sun in late winter.
Sometimes we let them go through dreams,
giving away their clothes,
keeping only the pocket knife or star quilt.

'Do what you have to,' we remember them saying.
And so we must do with them
who are tired from their effort to be dead,
still not sure where to go,
so they linger with us awhile
before their journey.

Sometimes we sleep well in the midst of terrible grief
or remember something funny they said.
They give these small gifts to us before they leave.
Then for no reason, months later,
we walk into a room unexpectedly filled with flowers
and cry totally, knowing they are dead and forever.

It's good.
Our weeping lessens their memory of us
and they begin to travel more easily,
doing their work, which is to be dead,
not for us or anyone.
We feel better just speaking
of the past,
that too without them.

4. Submission to Single Rooms

The bedroom hovers at dusk
simple as a child practicing piano.
It's summer.
I lie naked on the rose chenille and smoke.

The first time we drank a little whiskey
before our shadow show
ignited like flint sparks.

In the photo on the vanity my mother
looks amazingly young.
I break my vow and think of you often.
Why I left. Because pain rose above us
seeking its own level like a water table.

5. Submission to Silence

How terrible to say nothing,
like an old woman undressing.

It's a stone turned tumor,
more silent than dead meat in a butcher's window,
or a shoe repair filled with the worn gloves of feet.
And sometimes we drive through the white space of sand
noticing the blue line of water clean as opened wrists.

I fry pork for supper.
We sit across from each other,
eating in the silence.

Syphilis Prior to Penicillin

The United States Coast Guard had a
hospital for it in New York until 1952.
My doctor said if you knew syphilis,
you knew medicine because it
perfectly imitated other diseases.
That in the last stages when it went rampant,
(besides their minds)
sailors would lose a nose or ear,
the disease mimicking leprosy.
And it was never cured or stabilized
so the sailors carried themselves as
weapons into every port.

The whores could never really tell either
for they were eaten with it too.
Those who knew their condition
often banded together
trying not to infect others with
a 'taste for the mud' as the French say.

They were a cavalier and doomed lot,
trying to hold back the dawn
in their foreign hotels,
where the night porters filled rooms
with verbena and gardenias
to hide the cooking smells of sulphur ointments

At the last there were signs they couldn't hide.
The motor nerves giving way so they walked with

odd flickering steps. That's why Amelia and Rose Montana
would sit the evening through playing mah-jongg,
and the old sailors, Paul and James,
rarely asked the whores to dance.

for DAVID WOJAHN

Oshi

Oshi has a very large Buddha in him, one that can change the air into scented flowers. He used to be Tommy Whalen from Indianapolis but he had his eyes cut to look Japanese. He got started out in San Francisco in the early days when Buddha consciousness was just rising out there and people were still slipping pork in the seaweed soup.

At seventeen he did drag in a place called The Gay Deceiver and was billed as 'The Boy With The Face Like The Girl Next Door.' The owners paid him almost nothing and kept him strung out on hash in a little room above the bar, like a bad detective novel.

Somehow Oshi found the Zen community and started sitting za-zen. He collected 'mad money' from the state for being strung out. It's free out there if you're crazy enough. Oshi breathed hash and gin through the Buddha. Buddha breathed light and air through Oshi. It all changed his mind to indigo. Buddha consciousness rose in him until he didn't feel like the broken piano at the bar anymore.

Now thirty years later he has a permanent room at the bath house and prays for young boys. Doesn't sit anymore. Said he became realized ten years ago with a young hustler from Akron, Ohio who told him he could stop flying, just lay back and touch ground.

Old Oshi, very round now, jet black wig, looks like a retired Buddha in his cheap wash-and-wear kimonos. He's a graceful old gentleman Buddha. Buys everyone drinks. Gives away joints. Always high. Always lighting joss sticks. As he says, 'Giving things is just a way of getting on with everyone, you know, the universe and everything. It's like passing on the light.'

He told me once when he sang Billie Holiday's 'Blue Monday' at The Gay Deceiver they used an amber spot and he wore a strapless lamé gown, beaded on his eyelashes, lacquered his nails, and the people cried.

Returning

Ruth, how noticeably you've aged,
the stroke leaving a medical patch
over your left eye.

I visit and you notice me slightly,
staring mostly at old re-runs,
or perhaps thinking of a man named Irving
who's driven up from the Dells for the past 20 years
to engage you both
in what you once were.

Some quiz show starts and
it's the only time you look right at me.
'Do you watch this one? It's good.'
The room's blued by TV.
A late August night, close as sulphur.
Everything's overripe,
the vacation where I stay too long
with old friends who liked me better
the way I was.

She dozes.
I remember her ancient name means compassion.
Ruth, who has gathered herself among sorrow
so quietly she refuses to touch this world again.

I leave the blue and camphor smells,
still hearing the TV in the distance.
Everything falls like slate gray swans in the night,
with asters burning to what's not there.

Sunday Snow

I walk around the cold rooms trying to remember
if it's sorrow or light that brings me to her small face
and ribs I want to play like forbidden chimes.
I walk the cold alone and admit it's sorrow
that brings me to the light.

My emptiness festers into a Sunday forever.
I want to believe in the little girl
beyond my needs for darkness.
I want to bring her into light like a tablet washed by sun,
where she can finger up each contour of my despair.

A gray mist comes from the gray park below as I write:
'A gray mist comes from the gray park below.
The little girl rides a naked horse gray,
rides blood red over his back
in the gray park, in the gray naked snow.'

It is Sunday.
It is Sunday forever and begins to snow.
I am going into the snow
as I have wanted to do for years.

A Colored Girl

Me waiting on a bus.
She comes down the street nearly dark,
plum colored taffeta dress, ruffled top,
the way a light wind does on a hot night.

She stops by me, very, very high.
I'm nervous because I think
she's trying to hustle me,
so I ask her for a smoke.
She says sure,
asks if I'm interested in some fun.
I say I'm Gay.
She's lost complete interest and
is digging in this huge bag for a smoke.
Pulls out a bent Salem and even lights it for me.

I ask her how's work.
She says slow on the southside.
I look close at her,
scared because she's beautiful and made up,
rouge, marcelled hair, nail polish,
and finally say,
'You look like a colored girl.'
She laughs and says,
'I know baby, johns your age like that.'
She walks on and I say, 'Be careful now, hear?'

for B. R. L.

Dying Out

I love the cambric night snowing down First Avenue
and the heaven of being near things I know,
my apartment, the old rugs and chair, the moons
of my nails above which I write.

And the snow in distant woods where animals
give silently all
and everything into dying—their fossils in spring,
the jonquil and pure bone.

I'm no more alone than usual
with this perfect history of snowing
so quietly without people.
I've left so many this year
who've felt too comfortable with my old design.
Because I want another life rinsed new in middle age,
the way a hard sickness changes a person.
The way snow changes the billboards
by my drugstore to read VANQUISH PAIN and
RELIEF FROM THE ORDINARY.

I don't want forgiveness from people,
only to be seen from another way,
like the back of a sculpture,
perhaps the nape of a neck or an open helpless palm,
some familiar form viewed from another direction.

Vinegar

In his underwear
a man writes a poem in a motel room
then holds it to a mirror.
The poem begins to translate:
'. . . an oyster white cup on the ebony sill . . .'
Then he writes 'vinegar' and 'old' and begins to cry.

Having matched these objects with something unnamed
the way a smouldering fire can sometimes tell us
who we are, he continues.
The towel and the cup and everything else he sees
burn in vinegar
like the edge of himself.

He dozes at the desk
and dreams of living without danger
or the fear of death.
Dreams of a laundry room in summer
with its cool bleach smell, hands lifting
in Fels Naphtha.
A bowl of bluing . . . simple enough
as though heaven could be so.

A car sounds somewhere and he wakes
nearly dreaming of a Black neighborhood
where a barber chair sits in a front yard,
and a train almost runs through someone's house
by Estelle's Café and Beauty Parlour.

The Arc-Welder's Blue

Only silence can make it all,
a blue towel, vinegar, and salt fire.
Silence toward totality,
the way giant turtles sum themselves up at death,
going from what they were into the sea,
their claws scratching RUTH and HARROW
on the sand.

Words from silence so excellent at genesis
like a sexual flower,
come through an ill-formed life
where no metaphor of soaring bird will do,
only a coal yard in late sun blazed on black rock.

If silence is possible
it forges the arc-welder's blue
for the corporeal and daily
so we look away and are still drawn.
Silence, submission to the ordinary,
like a memory of a laundry room in summer,
chartreuse light and bluing smell, mingling
with coffee upstairs and more, but distant
and childish, gone.

Naming

Old woman, my mother,
let's do the world again you and me,
this time in the desert outside Gallup, New Mexico
where the sky's as bright as cut ribbons.

We'd take long walks in our clay life
where nothing's taught and I'd learn everything,
like stopping the wind
by pinning a small shell in your hair, that certain
days in spring are called
mother-in-law weather.
Here is a weed to smoke for dreams
and that's called 'hawk,'
a flutter from the canyon rim.

Old woman, don't die.
Take me to your first words again,
to say there are plants that live as people,
that certain animals carry dreams,
that the hawk is itself where the canyon drops to air.

'Look son, there's a word for getting
off work late at night, your collar
damp with sweat, and one
for loneliness that starts at the base of the spine.
There's a word for mystery,
the morning rose on the kitchen table
opening all on its own,
almost green at the base of the bud,
quietly doing the way it knows to.'

Old woman, my mother,
so full of sickness it becomes acquaintance,
don't die. The world is nearly empty for me.
Take me near your river of first words again.
'Look son, this is stone.
Here is flower.
Here between my legs you entered the world.
Call it "door."
Look son, another flower called going away, and this
is called too soon.'

for MARIE WHITE

Uncollected Work

An Autobiographical Fragment

I don't know how to begin this or even if I want to begin it, the story of my life, because I'm a failure, and very unhappy person. That means a lot of words would whine a great deal, but I think the life is unusual because it's full of romantic deception that I've acted upon. Through most of my young life I was on drugs of one sort or another that made the romance seem real enough, and because I was (and am) mentally ill, it all seemed real to me. So I lived a fiction as I do now. I was a half-rate ballet corps dancer, a soldier, a poet of some small merit, and wanderer of the earth, and a self-hater. But how does one begin all this, a little house simple enough on the prairie, humble origins where the virtues of honesty and forthrightness bored me . . . no. My origins were humble enough; I never rose from them. Today at forty-three I had to count all the pennies in a jar because it's Columbus Day and the banks are closed and I came up with six bucks and some change. I want enough to go to the bathhouse this afternoon.

Again, the origins. I lived in a yellow house in Indianapolis with a mother who always seemed old to me and mostly without joy, though she remains in my life, as with most homosexual men, the most constant and strongest figure. I had a father who seemed no more than a shadow; he worked nights as a gateman for the gas-works and would leave me a small present in his smoking stand in the morning, an orange or a little toy, and that's about all I remember of him, until I was eleven and my family forced me to go to the hospital and see him. It seemed he was lying on a table in General Hospital, nearly naked, a sheet over his middle, and glass tubes seemed to protrude from him in all directions and the white sheet seemed so white in the gray room of the city charity hospital, and my father seemed so removed, as though he'd gone elsewhere, the way the dying often do. Later I was to see a photo of Spain's great bullfighter, Manolito, directly at his death. He was on a strange makeshift operating table and completely covered with a white sheet save for his head, and because the camera was old the white of the sheet burned the photo so it seemed to glow, and the men about Manolito all in black suits and bowlers were posed before the camera. Posed! They were grinning, or staring directly into the lens. Not one looked at Manolito, the great flower of Spain, who had already gone out, who had the grace in death not to pose, who seemed to be luminous in his death as he was luminous in his life.

But my father seemed removed, too. I didn't really know him there on the table so thinned by the disease, having been in a coma for days, but I didn't know him in life either. He was a large shadow that I feared. The only images that stay with me now are the summer nights on weekends when he'd be home, and sit on the front porch smoking his cigar. The sound of the porch swing when we lived on Winter Avenue, and then the glider when we lived on Rural Street, and how he'd not say much, just the glow of the cigar, and the yellow bug light on the porch and the moths.

He and my mother never married, which made him more of a stranger. She'd had three children by another man who left her, and so she raised them herself, and then she met my father, who was married to an invalid and so could never really marry my mother. But these are legends and half-lies and I'm not sure of the truth, because they were extracted from an alcoholic cousin of mine for a few drinks I'd given her. All I know was he was a shadow and silent and his world was ruled by women. And they must have been women who hated him, or hated men in general: my mother to this day I believe still hates men.

All she could remember was their cruelty and strength that she must have felt helpless against. Her maiden name was Baley and she lived with her mother and father on Irish Hill, the very poor laboring part of Indianapolis, and she was English blood living among all the Irish laborers. My grandfather, who I never met, was another shadow in my life, a brick layer and a house painter and a drunk, and so there were always strange drunk men around the house and she'd say "sometimes they'd try to get dirty with me" and she'd have to throw them out. But all this is shadow again. The real truth is locked in our bones, in the history of our bodies, and is never really spoken. The story of our lives is so far locked down in us that it has no words, and that is the most honest history. Not that my father was a stranger and smoked his cigar and looked long out into the night or that my mother hated men and said two days after we buried him, "It's a terrible thing to say, Jim, but we're better off without him," and the night he died, she put his pillow in the closet, and slept from then on in the middle of the bed, this is recordable history. What we all feel and never say is the honest truth.

I am the history. Forty-three, dying of a bad heart, and a moderately good, moderately known poet. But all that lies, too. You ask me who I am and I say, I'm a man something like my father, always looking away, always looking hard out into the long night, I am my mother working hard as any man to keep the two of us alive after his death and hating the struggle and hating the males who cause the struggle. No, this isn't who I am either; I am the results of these emotions. These are the nameless, the voiceless and soundless that built me where there was no father to become, no mirror in which to look, only the need to call *father* into every street, every bar, every desperate hour of my life. Who has the right to call any man father? That is burden indeed and yet what son doesn't want to call that name as though someone could help or understand?

Again, this becomes a lie. When it's voiced it's a lie.

My father would disappear for long hours on weekends. He'd walk downtown. He must have been very lonely. He must have wanted desperately to talk to someone. He was to my knowledge totally severed from his family, his origins. I don't even know where he came from. Only his real name wasn't White. It was Broadell, Roscoe Broadell, which means "the fastest horse of the broad valley." And when we buried him, we buried him under the name White. There were so many lies in my family, or more correctly, there were so many truths to choose from, and each had part of the truth in it, but generally what was silent was the larger part of the truth, and the larger history of myself.

I wondered where my father went when he disappeared. I'm a very sexual man and I always dreamed that he sought flesh in some way. Even the flesh of the burlesque house. That would be a mysterious connection with my father for I've spent a large part of my life seeking every conceivable sexual act with men, but somewhere in my stomach it all says it was never the right man. Somewhere deep down, I have to tell you my father was never dead enough so I tried to find him through other men, and of course it was never the right man. As the Psalm says, "like as the hart desireth the waterbrook, so longeth my soul after thee. . . ." Even to say *villain* of my father is easy enough, that he was a bastard, that I was his bastard. Those are simple ways to define a person, but to say that he was a part of my loneliness and I must have been a living part of his despair is to say it more clearly.

.ᴗ

I remember very little about the yellow house on Winter Avenue. I remember a dairy that had a silver tower and railroad tracks. All through my childhood I remember railroads because we lived so close to them and how they thrilled my childhood because those great beautiful, loud, clanging, steaming black things were going somewhere . . . somewhere that I would never know, and I'd look at those trains going down the track and my heart would long for the distance those train drivers must have known, those grand old fellows who always waved. And late at night, in another house when I was older and we lived by the coal yard, the trains came very close and would shake the house, shake the windowpanes, and again would shake my heart, wake me from my sleep with the most warm comfort and their whistles were like something searching the night. The train whistles calling out became me. There was something about them that would stay forever though I knew my life would not. My father talking softly late into the night in the bedroom wouldn't last, or my world of things wouldn't last. I felt only the trains and the end of the world were the two inevitable elements of life. The beautiful great trains and the flaming balls of fire that would destroy the world before I was grown. I remember asking my mother if the end of the world was so, if it would really happen, and she would pause and say yes, she really believed it would happen, and it always terrified me, because it happened from sin, my sin, and the sin of those around me, and there was nothing to be done about it. I would sit on the back steps with my dog Jerry in the very late day and think, This is the time it will happen, when the sky is nearly red. I would look at the conveyor belts and machines in the coal yard that looked like giant praying mantises or prehistoric dinosaurs and I thought this is the way the world will end, these strange shapes taking form, the world in flames, my mother and father and sisters and brother dying in flames, everything going up in flames because we were alive and to live meant simply to sin and there was nothing that could be done about it. I would sit on the back porch steps and cry with my dog and think often about this and talk to my young friends about it. Now I realize we were experiencing the first atomic blast in our psyches five or six years before it would happen.

I remember the day after my father's burial my mother sitting at the kitchen table trying to collect herself, which meant biting her lip and looking out the window and saying "I don't quite know how we're going to make it," and then she cried. And the next day she went down and found a job at Rite's Clothing and Jewelry, Easy Terms. My mother and I to this day have a private joke about "easy terms": whenever something is obviously crooked or impossible we look at each other and say, "easy terms."

That period in my life was rather fantastic in Indianapolis, or it seemed to me fantastic. The stories my mother brought home from work and that the store was right across the street from the Mutual Burlesque House, which had a second-floor stairway that led right into the bar next door called The Stage Door. There are rumors that late at night James Whitcomb Riley would view the women at the Mutual Burlesque then drink himself into oblivion at The Stage Door. The burlesque fascinated me. My mother always had stories of the strippers who would come to the store to buy clothes "on terms" and how they seemed decent enough even though they were still cheap.

On Saturdays I'd stay at my brother's house and we'd pick my mother up in the snow in front of Rite's and the iron bars would be slowly closing in front of the windows. My mother was in her salesperson black dress. And the snow and all the Christmas things glittering the streets and the burlesque with a star billed in front, her tits being slowly covered over with snow. EVELYN WEST, WITH HER FIFTY THOUSAND DOLLAR TREASURE CHEST. My mother would talk about some of the "stars" coming into the store. "My God, she was every bit as old as I am, and bleached hair so stiff it looked like a haystack! But she seemed nice though. Just as easy to talk to as anyone you'd want to know."

My mother always had an aura of acceptance around her, a kind of liberal spirit. I don't know if in the past she decided things weren't quite as proper as people carry on about, or because she felt her son is homosexual, or because she went against the grain of what must have been a pretty Victorian society to not marry and have an illegitimate son. My mother was never too condemning of the bizarre. I think it's because we were a bit bizarre. With her as well as the rest of the family, the truth of something may always be there as long as it's never voiced.

My older sister Gert lived with a drunken man for thirty years and never cried out for help until finally her heart exploded from grief at not saying what she wanted to say: that she was in pain all those years, and my heart has done the same, and in writing these words I too look at the men in my life and three-fourths of those I've loved have either been drunks or drug-dependent, and part of my love has been to take care of them just like the women in my family have had to take care of drunken men: pull off their shoes, listen to them wail their sorrow, tend their anger.

One of the things that so frightened me when I drank and if I drink now is rage in my sleep. I roar and I've done so since I was a young boy. The underneath in me is terrible, the three-quarters below the iceberg, fearful and dark and large, and always on the surface I've appeared a gentle and kind man. That's one of the useful lies of my life. I think that's one of the useful lies of being a homosexual: we mostly appear as we are not and it is a way to mask our terrible anger. Don't be confused when you see a swishy homosexual man being campy and outrageous: you're observing anger, and it's anger and outrage the homosexual is often not aware of and so he takes his feelings of violence and frustration out by breaking the icons.

I watched the city of Indianapolis change from a soldier's town during WWII back into a mild and ominously conservative, unimaginative place. But during the wars, both WWII and Korean, there was a carelessness and ease that made it comfortable to live in, and anyone who was as drawn to sin as myself found the whole atmosphere of a downtown area dedicated to taking the money of transient troops for "a little French fun" was really my cup of tea. A relief from the tight and closed atmosphere of my house with my mother, which was dark in a way that I'm sure has marked all my life. My mother was in a great deal of pain. She must have felt enormous rage and abandonment at having been left alone to raise a small boy and so she must have wanted me to know how hard life was, how difficult it was for us, and how men had basically caused all this, and so from her I developed this fear, but also this attraction.

But the time during the wars: Indianapolis had a strip on Illinois Street that I've seldom seen equaled, or perhaps I was simply young and it was my first, but it lit up the sky like a zircon ring bought at a pawnshop on a Saturday night. For some reason, everyone called the strip "the levee." It was just a section of bars, the bus station, cheap hotels, a great cheap chili parlor called Blacker's, where if you could stand eating the food and didn't throw up, you would realize that it was great food . . . . The strip represented a kind of freedom for everyone. The service men had that ease from being transient and also that fear of not knowing what lay ahead for them, so they were a doomed and cavalier and casual lot, and the whores out on the street were by and large an easy going group, but there was about it too a feeling of danger. A feeling that everyone had to force a lot into those weekend nights. For the service men, it must have been wanting to stay with a girl one more time before something happened to them that they had no control over, and so there were a lot of beds squeaking in the hotels up and down the levee, and for the women there was easy money to be made quick, and for the nightclubs it was letting the good times roll. It was a desperate moment in our lives that everyone took advantage of, because we, that damn old cheap Midwestern town and everyone in it, were trying to say goodbye to those young men, those sweet flowers, and it seems the only way we know how to do it from the time of year one was to get a troop drunk and fucked and roll him if you can before his ass is shipped to Germany or Japan or Korea or

Viet Nam. It's a terrible way to say goodbye to those we love, it's a terrible way to deal with our fear.

Looking back on it I wish I'd had the courage not to have gone to the Army. To have gone to jail, but I was too afraid. I was afraid because I was gay and for me saying I was gay was something you didn't do in the fifties. There were nights I spent on troop ships packed with seasick soldiers after I'd finished basic training and was being sent to Germany when I wondered if I was a coward and I always answered yes. I remember something very wonderful about my trip over. We were all to sleep on berths that were stacked very high, and they were stacked so close you couldn't turn over. You had to strap yourself in, and there was another troop that slept right next to you. They made sure we slept head to head, not head to foot. I'm sure I would have sucked this guy's cock if the latter had been so. We didn't know each other, barely spoke. I can't even remember what he looks like now. He seemed attractive, all I remember is that he seemed moderately attractive. In the night, after I'd get off guard duty on the late watch I'd crawl into my bunk and hear him sleeping heavily. The large area where we all slept was very dark except for an occasional red exit light so we were all cast in shadows. We heard the pound of the sea and the cast of the ship was felt deeply in us. I'd crawl into my berth and strap myself in. About the third night after I'd gotten off watch, I went to my berth, and noticed the troop I slept next to was losing his blanket. I pulled it up around his shoulders, and we woke up the next morning holding hands. And we held hands or touched shoulders or touched in some way until the voyage was finished in Germany. There in the night we touched and I wondered was I a coward and I knew in my bones I must have been, but I new it in my bones that we all must have been, and I loved him in some small way in the dark as he must have loved me. Was he homosexual too? I don't know. I don't think so. I think he was simply like myself: afraid of what lay ahead, and somehow touching us made us less afraid.

Looking back on it, we were afraid of the night. The men on the ship, the men of my life, myself: afraid of what the large and dark night might bring. All of us breathing in the great ship being taken to places we'd never heard of, and I wonder now if that isn't sometimes the one connection that all men have in common, that we are afraid of the dark. Even the man who slept next to me. We slept as close as lovers all the way across the ocean and very late at night we would hold each other in some fear of the dark. I never spoke to the man during the day, but it was as though our hands could offer some small solace against the unknown that lay ahead.

.⌣

(Don't be afraid, Jim. Sometimes this will hurt you but there is also great beauty in your life. Don't be afraid, Jim, or if you're afraid, just go on and do what you do have to do: tell it, tell the story.)

October 8, 1979–October 11, 1979

Whitefish Lake, Late Summer, 1978

It stays in my mind we've all gotten old.
Darkness spreading each year, we continue
fearing death, kinder, humiliated by money.

We don't talk about the lake's other life
full of the mystical fire of nameless birds
or boats holding lovers in the slow sun.
Even the small island where children knew
Indian spirits lived, casting razor-blue shadows
in their loneliness.

Life's no longer that beautiful.
We've had to stretch things too far
and can't pretend even mild gentility.
We keep nearly as large a garden,
we walk nearly the same distance and
we dream almost never.

The lake now purple, no
loons or thrilling ripples before dark.
We've pushed everything to go further than
was meant.

Tonight we look hard at the island and see
the blue figures ready for departure, burning
their souls, sprinkling ashes to the wind,
common rocks, the trumpets of tiger lilies.
Tonight for once we dream the same dream, and
call out over and over: "Please wait for us. Don't
leave us. We're nearly ready. Don't go. Wait!
Don't leave without us!"

Sleep

Let me sleep for us all
further than our aging.
To the elmed season,
sun found and cradled
within the browning shell.

We'll sleep tonight
who've tightened nerves into years
with our faces of electricity.

Let's sleep into a flesh fall nearly innocent
where warmth is brought by skin and breath.
We'll wrap our hair into the swirled white
of hill line and fur.

Traveler,
gone too far,
return and rest.

James L. White was born in Indianapolis, Indiana, in 1936. At the age of sixteen, he began his training as a classical ballet dancer and was awarded a scholarship to the American Ballet Theater School. He danced for ten years in America and Germany. After his dance career, he attended universities in Indiana and Colorado, and then taught among Navajo tribes in New Mexico and Arizona. White came to Minnesota to develop a creative writing program for Chippewa children through the Minnesota Writers in the Schools Program. He was the author of four books of poetry: *Divorce Proceedings* (1972), *A Crow's Story of Deer* (1974), *The Del Rio Hotel* (1975), and *The Salt Ecstasies* (1982). In 1978, White was awarded the Bush Foundation Fellowship for Poetry. He lived in Minneapolis until his death in 1981.

Mark Doty, editor of the Graywolf Poetry Re/View Series, is the author of eight books of poems, including *Fire to Fire: New and Selected Poems*, which won the 2008 National Book Award. He is also the author of four books of nonfiction prose, including *Heaven's Coast*, which received the PEN/Martha Albrand Award. He teaches creative writing and literature at Rutgers University and lives in New York City.

The Salt Ecstacies has been typeset in Berling, a font design by Karl-Erik Forsberg in 1951 for the Berlingska Stilgjuteriet in Sweden. Book design by Wendy Holdman, composition by BookMobile Design and Publishing Services, Minneapolis, Minnesota, and manufactured by Versa Press on acid-free paper.